THE WORLD ART TOUR

Dance

Architecture
Clothing and Fashion
Culinary Arts
Dance
Decorative Arts
Drawing and Painting
Festivals
Sculpture

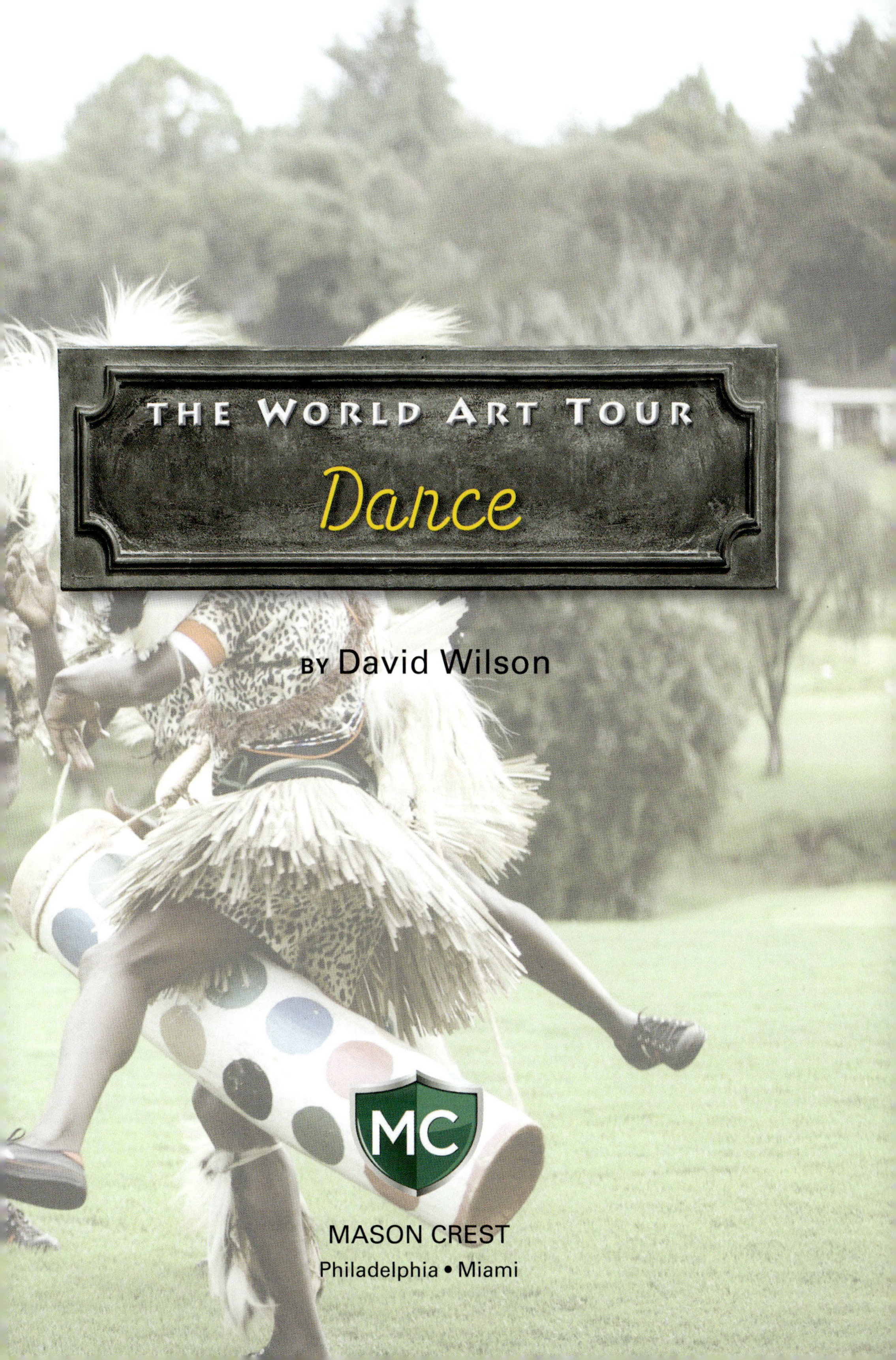

THE WORLD ART TOUR

Dance

BY David Wilson

MASON CREST
Philadelphia • Miami

Mason Crest
450 Parkway Drive, Suite D
Broomall, PA 19008
(866) MCP-BOOK (toll free)
www.masoncrest.com

Printed in the United States of America

First printing
9 8 7 6 5 4 3 2 1

Series ISBN: 978-1-4222-4283-4
Hardcover ISBN: 978-1-4222-4287-2
ebook ISBN: 978-1-4222-7534-4

Cataloging-in-Publication Data is available on file
at the Library of Congress.

Developed and Produced by Print Matters Productions, Inc.
(www.printmattersinc.com)

Cover and Interior Design by Tom Carling, Carling Design, Inc.

CONTENTS

INTRODUCTION

The urge to move whenever one hears music, whether it is a full orchestra or the simple beat of a drum, is so universal among the human psyche that there is no culture on earth that does not have its own traditions of dance. Dance is a unique art form in that it is almost entirely physical, relying on the person to create a distinct type of expression and transmit it to an audience to tell a story, demonstrate a skill, or express joy through physical motion. Dance can be as simple as one person weaving to a beat or as complicated as a dozen performers acting in perfect synchronization.

The history of dance goes back as far as the history of humanity itself. Rock art from prehistoric sites portrays dancing figures, whereas statues made from clay, rock, and precious stone have survived the centuries to tell stories of dance in ancient Indian, Chinese, Greek, and Egyptian cultures. It is probable that the oldest instruments discovered, flutes carved from animal bones tens of thousands of years ago, led our ancestors to dance as well as play and sing.

Most of the dances discussed in this chapter fall into one of several major categories. Many are folk dances, performed by peasants and farmers at ceremonies like weddings and funerals. Others are tribal dances, specific to one ethnic or cultural group, where young boys become men in initiation ceremonies, or shamans and priests call on the spirits to send good fortune, rain, or herds of animals. Other dances (including many modern dances) are mating rituals, meant to demonstrate the physical strength and dexterity of a man, sometimes in contrast to the reserve or restraint of a woman. Yet there are many more types of dances, including quite a few that have no purpose other than to express emotion.

Dance can be organic and improvised, relying on no explicit set of movements, or it can be highly technical and choreographed, forcing participants to practice until their bodies are so attuned to the beat that they will not make a mistake. Some dances carry strict penalties for failing. The *baining* fire dance, for example, requires participants to leap through a scorching bonfire. One misstep can be disastrous, or even fatal. By contrast, a spiritual dance like the Japanese kabuki dance is meant to invoke the favor of gods and spirits, meaning that a misstep is not physically harmful but can call down misfortune on an entire community.

Oftentimes, dance involves an elaborate costume. This costume does not need to be complex; in the case of the Arabic belly dance, in fact, less is more. A national dance often requires a national costume, as is the case for the Mexican *jarabe tapatío* (the hat dance), where men wear large sombreros while women wear flowing dresses. The costume of a dance may help to tell a story by assigning a quality to the participant—a hero, a suitor, a god, an animal, or a rebel. Virtually all costumes for dance are bright and energetic, meant to stimulate the senses just as much as the dancers themselves.

The music that accompanies global dance varies in many ways. For several dances, participants need nothing more than a drum to keep a beat, whereas some do not feature any instruments at all, requiring only that the audience clap or chant as they go. Yet the instruments for some dance music may be just as important as the dance moves themselves. Can you imagine swing dancing without a jazz saxophone, or breakdancing without a hip-hop beat to back it up?

A common factor in many dances throughout the world is a division of role and gender. Many dances are men-only or women-only, whereas others are partner dances involving a man and a woman, with the man leading and the woman following. This gendered division is likely as old as dance itself, especially because dance in many cultures is synonymous with love, marriage, and attraction. Even so, many traditional dances meant for all-male or all-female pairings or groupings have opened up in modern times to accommodate both genders, although some cultures remain particularly strict about the division of the sexes and will not allow one or the other to participate.

People dance for a wide variety of reasons and emotions. Throughout this chapter you'll see how dance correlates to happiness, sadness, hope, fear, glory, and pride. So long as music continues to play, people will continue to dance, and the beat will go on as it has for thousands and thousands of years.

KEY TERMS

Accent: The stress put on any one beat in music, usually meant to signal to dancers that they must pivot or move in a new way.

Backspin: Putting weight on the upper body and pushing away with the hands or legs to create a spinning motion.

Ballroom dance: A highly formalized dance with a focus on choreography, with little or no improvisation.

Battle: A hip-hop or rap competition involving singing, chanting, and/or dancing.

Choreography: Specific dance movements, usually practiced intensely, that must be followed to properly execute the dance itself.

Chorus: A group of singers.

Circle dance: A dance where participants arrange themselves in a circle, sometimes with a dancer or pair moving into the center.

Continuity: The act of moving consistently from step to step in a dance, without pause.

Costume: Clothing worn by dance participants.

Dance floor: The physical stage, whether crafted or natural, for a dance.

Drop: The support of most or all of the follower's body weight by the leading partner.

Elevation: The vertical aspect of dance, involving leaping or holding upright.

First position: The beginning of a dance, usually referring to ballet.

Follow, or follower: The dancer in a partner pair who does not direct the movement and follows the motion.

Gyrate: Rotate a body part.

Heelspin: A pivot move where a dancer puts weight on the heel and turns.

Improvisation: Movement that is made up on the spot by a dancer, without adherence to any formalized route.

Jig: A simple song in 6/8 time.

Lead, or leader: The dancer in a partner pair who takes the initiative and directs the movement.

Line: A dimension of body running from head to toe that dancers must achieve with movement.

Line dance: A dance where all participants arrange themselves in lines, usually two lines facing each other.

One step: A dance with no change in rhythm.

Rhythm: Beat of music that dictates how and when dancers will move.

Tempo: Speed of music.

CHAPTER 1 AFRICA

Because the first evidence of human evolution comes to us from Africa, it is probable that dance itself originated on this continent. Today, the world's second largest continent (by both size and population) boasts a huge variety of dance and music, contemporary and traditional. Many African dances have cultural roots as mating dances and/or warrior dances; some have changed drastically over time, but others have had few, if any, alterations to the central theme.

THE SOUTH AFRICAN ZULU TRIBE: A WAR DANCE NOW USED FOR CELEBRATION

The Zulu tribe of South Africa may be the most well known of all African tribes, due to their fierce resistance against white imperialism during the 1800s. They are also among the most populous, at some 12 million strong. The word *Zulu* means "people of Heaven," and today about half the population of South Africa can speak or understand their language.

The *indlamu* Zulu dance has been an integral part of their culture's history. It reflects an evolution from historical war dances that are no longer performed, given that the Zulu no longer have a martial society. Today, weddings and major occasions account for contemporary *indlamu* dance, having been transformed from a war dance into a dance of celebration.

A group of men from the Zulu tribe perform the* indlamu *dance at a wedding.

Zulu men in their warrior attire.

Although it is no longer a war dance, *indlamu* still involves two members of the Zulu community in full warrior attire. These men wear protective *amabeshu* hoods of thick leather skins, head rings and headdresses, rattles on their ankles, and weapons like spears and "knobkerrie" clubs. *Indlamu* represents a great physical challenge to dancers: Men use their weapons in the dance, rhythmically fighting imaginary foes.

Like for many other African tribal dances, the primary musical instruments of *indlamu* are drums, although whistles are used as well. It is a dance of precision timing—both participants must hit their feet on the ground in exact time with the beat. They then must be able to lift their feet entirely above their head to stamp downward. Control of the body is paramount, as both dancers are expected to be in sync with each other while also demonstrating good form when they strike with their weapons at certain intervals. Usually at a Zulu wedding, the *indlamu* dance will be followed by another gender-specific dance, the *ingoma*, where women dance in time while men clap.

KIZOMBA MEANS "PARTY" IN ANGOLA

The word *kizomba* means "party" in the Angolan language, and there's no doubt that the catchy beat of the Kizomba dance makes people want to have a good time. *Kizomba* originated in the 1980s and exploded onto the scene in Angola during the 1990s after the singer Eduardo Paim featured the dance in his songs. It is famous for its electric percussion, which provides a clear beat to dance partners, although the beat is not necessarily fast.

Kizomba is a partner dance where both dancers perform very close to one another with overly exaggerated movements, somewhat akin to salsa dancing.

Kizomba *requires dance partners to perform close to one another with exaggerated movements.*

Kizomba has gone global! Pictured here, groups gather in Washington, D.C., to perform the Angolan dance.

The leader, usually the male partner, must direct the motion and the pace, holding his partner close as they twist and turn. Both dancers must focus on smooth pivots and controlled movements, keeping each other tight and close as they move their feet. Even so, it's considered a dance appropriate for family and children. By contrast, a version of the dance known as *karaxinha* takes the intimacy even closer and ramps up the tempo; in overwhelmingly Christian Angola, *karaxinha* dance is considered only appropriate for two people already in a romantic relationship.

Kizomba has become so influential throughout Angola and southern Africa that it has changed the traditional dance, the samba, making the slower dance much more up-tempo in some modern interpretations. It's gone global, furthermore, and dance studios across the world teach *kizomba*, putting their unique interpretations on the gyrating movements. Some critics claim that *kizomba* must remain uniquely Angolan: A 2012 movement called "Kizomba on the Streets" sought to entrench *kizomba* in the national culture while also defending it against foreign alterations. Portuguese is the official language of *kizomba* music, and the dance is most often associated with other former Portuguese colonies like Cape Verde and Mozambique.

THE MAASAI PERFORM A JUMPING DANCE TO WOO A BRIDE

The Maasai people inhabit Kenya and Tanzania, two of the most visited places in Africa, and their *adamu*, or jumping dance, has become nearly as popular a tourist attraction as the savanna's elephants and lions. It's often mentioned as a deceptive dance: It looks easy to jump up in the air in time with the beat, but visitors find they're incapable of jumping as high as the tribe members themselves.

Although the dance may look simple, visitors find it difficult to keep up with the Maasai men during the traditional jumping dance.

Adamu is a warrior dance performed by men, supported by women. It is unique in several ways, most notably by the fact that the Maasai do not use musical instruments of any kind, instead using their voices to make music and keep time. It begins with the warriors of the tribe (all adult men—the Maasai have a famously intense rite of passage for their boys, requiring them to spend 10 years away from the main village) forming a circle as women sing to provide the musical rhythm. Two men step into the circle, and the dance begins. They jump higher and higher each time while chanting in time with the circle, growing in intensity while they leap into the air. They wear a simple garment called a *shuka*, an animal skin or bolt of cotton, usually dyed red to blend in with the color of the earth.

Like many other African tribal dances, the *adamu* is primarily a show of physical strength. It is a mating dance that takes place during the ceremony of Eunoto, a time when young men become warriors and leaders in their tribe, having passed their tests of strength and determination. By jumping as high as they can, these new warrior graduates show off

The women of the Maasai provide the song that men dance and jump to during the Adamu.

their strength and virility to impress potential brides. The ceremony can last for days, meaning that warriors with endurance have the best chance to take home a wife. It's a moment that the Maasai practice for years before the event, because it is often a defining moment in their lives.

The Maasai Lion Hunt Separates the Men from the Boys

Many coming-of-age tests are imposed throughout the tribes of Africa, but perhaps none are more famous or more rigorous than the Maasai lion hunt. Maasai boys can become men and warriors of the tribe only once they have achieved a number of requirements, including hunting a lion. Unlike modern big-game hunting, furthermore, the Maasai can use only a simple spear and shield to protect them from one of the largest predators in the world. Due to dropping wildlife numbers, the Maasai today have put more restrictions on lion hunting.

ETHIOPIA'S *ESKITA* IS THE MOST DIFFICULT DANCE IN AFRICA

Literally meaning "rolling shoulders," but more commonly referred to as the "Snake Dance," Ethiopia's *eskita* is considered an integral part of Ethiopian culture—just as important as the *injera* flatbread served at every meal or the national sport of long-distance running. *Eskita* forms a part of any major Ethiopian social occasion, from holidays to weddings. It may be the most technically demanding dance in Africa—and perhaps in the entire world.

Dancers must maintain specific foot timings, hopping back and forth as their shoulders rotate, kicking out and pivoting their ankles at the same time as they clap. Dancers must also shake their chests and necks while rolling their shoulders as a further challenge. *Eskita* and other types of Ethiopian dance rely on traditional Ethiopian musical instruments, most notably the single-stringed *mesenko* and the five-stringed *krar* lyre, as well as drums and flutes.

Members of the Ethiopian Hamer tribe dance during a traditional ceremony.

IN THE CONGO, THE BEAT GOES ON DESPITE OBSTACLES

With a population of 10 million people, only a few cities in the entire world have a population greater than Kinshasa, the capital of the Democratic Republic of the Congo. Few cities have a more vibrant nightlife either, because Kinshasa is known around the world as a center of Congolese dance and music. Despite great poverty and a government clampdown on dancing (sometimes attacked as "deviancy"), dance culture flourishes here with stories of musicians who have to share instruments and orchestras who practice in empty warehouses.

The native Kinshasa singer Felix Wazekwa describes Congolese dance as both war and mating, mixing together combat and sex. Indeed, the Congolese *ndombolo* dance, famous for its fast movement and intense hip-swinging, has been banned in some African nations due to its "indecency." Though it's disliked by some, it has an international audience, with *ndombolo* songs becoming particularly popular in southern Africa.

Dancing is enjoyed by even the youngest citizens in the Democratic Republic of Congo. Pictured here, preschool students take part in singing and dancing.

ZAMBIA'S *SIPELU* BEGAN AS A MATING DANCE FOR WOMEN

In the Lozi language of Zambia, *sipelu* means "dancing swiftly." Performed with only a whistle as a musical instrument, the *sipelu* group dance relies on the voices of the crowd to build its tempo and reach frenzied heights, with each member clapping in time when they're not dancing themselves.

Sipelu is a traditional dance that was once a mating dance, although it turned the table on African gender norms by having women perform the dance rather than men. These eligible brides would impress potential husbands with their ability to keep time and move to the frenetic beat, as well as with *siziba* clothing that reflected their wealth and taste. However, any woman performing the *sipelu* was free to reject a suitor who attempted to pick her out of the crowd. Today, it's a genderless dance enjoyed by both men and women in Lozi culture.

The* sipelu *was originally performed by women to impress potential husbands.

Men keep the beat during assiko.

KEEPING THE BEAT WITH GLASS BOTTLES IN CAMEROON

Assiko is a partner dance popular in the southern regions of Cameroon in Central Africa. *Assiko* literally means "foot ground," and the tempo of the choreography emphasizes moving with your partner with exaggerated hip movements. Women wear flowing colorful skirts to show off their hips and demonstrate their ability to dance in time.

Assiko is often called the "bottle dance" because of the unique instruments used to keep the beat: Musicians will hit glass bottles with metal pieces to create rhythm, accompanying the sounds of a guitar, double bass, and drums with home-made music. This makes it popular throughout the country, because just about anyone can pick up a bottle and start keeping a beat for dancers.

Traditional intore *dancers.*

RWANDA'S MODERN WARRIOR DANCE

One of the most famous warrior dances of Africa, *intore* itself means "warrior" and has been a staple of Rwandan culture, performed at almost every major occasion throughout a person's life. Unlike other warrior dances, it is modern rather than ancient: It was first created in the 1800s as a way to train soldiers for the army. Despite its age, it has evolved, and movement and gestures in modern *intore* are symbolic of today's warfare as well as that of the past: An "eagle" dancer spreads his arms like a jet's wings to soar, whereas a "lion dancer" wears a thatch mane of fur and carries a simple spear and shield.

Women celebrate the dead in the famadihana *ceremony.*

A DANCE TO CELEBRATE THE DEAD IN MADAGASCAR

Unlike other African dances that celebrate love or martial vigor, the *famadihana* of Madagascar celebrates the dead. It is a funeral dance that means "turning of the bones." When a member of the family dies, the body is wrapped in a silken linen called *lambas* and taken to the family crypt. Surviving relatives dance around the body, while trumpets and clarinets provide a famously loud musical beat. The other bodies buried within the crypt may also be exhumed, taken out of their crypts, and given a fresh silken shroud so that relatives may dance with them. *Famadihana* ceremonies are believed to be centuries old, possibly a relic of South Asian funeral rites brought by the original colonists of Madagascar.

CHAPTER 2 ASIA

With a larger population than the rest of the world combined, Asia has a huge diversity in cultures, music, and dances. Asian dance spans the gamut from centuries-old traditional performances performed in small villages to modern moves that take place in big-city clubs.

INDIA'S THOUSANDS OF YEARS OF DANCE

Few places on earth have a longer history of dance than India. Although most modern associations of Indian dance involve Bollywood performances with dozens or even hundreds of backup dancers supporting the two main stars, Indian classical dance was first established in some of the oldest texts on Earth. The Sanskrit-language book *Natya Shastra*, written between 2,500 and 1,500 years ago, is one of the first published works in human history on the performing arts. It features commentary on eight dances that have become collectively known as *Shastriya Nritya*; the Indian Ministry of Culture has expanded the list to 10 that encompass classical dance.

Although some dances across the world involve little more than a musical rhythm and a pair of feet to match it, traditional Indian dance incorporates a huge variety of concepts into a proper performance. Participants must maintain the

***Kathak* dancers tell a story during their performances.**

Students perform the traditional* mohiniyattam *dance.

correct posture when standing and moving, the correct steps in time with the beat, the correct gestures of hands and limbs, the correct facial expressions, and the correct *rasa*, a term that means an aesthetic or emotion that cannot be described. Needless to say, Indian classical dance requires a great deal of study and commitment to master.

The 10 separate dance forms correspond to geographical regions. *Kathak* is a type of dance from Northwestern India that emphasizes storytelling, whereas *mohiniyattam* hails from the Southern coast and is strictly to be performed by solo female dancers.. However, all dances have three elements in common. The *nritta* performance of Indian dance emphasizes the technical accuracy, speed, and range of a dancer, with no subjective interpretation; the *nryita* is a slower movement meant to emphasize emotion and spirituality; and the *natyam* involves a group performance similar to a ballet, where all members act out a story line.

THE CHINESE DANCE WITH DRAGONS

The Chinese ring in their New Year with dancing, just as people do in English-speaking countries, but both their New Year and their dances are different from Western forms. The Chinese New Year is lunar rather than solar (meaning that it is measured by the progression of the moon's phases rather than the revolution of the Earth around the Sun), so it takes place on different days between January and February. One constant, however, is the famous dragon dance: a procession of dancers who lead a floatlike figure of a dragon on poles through public spaces and crowds to bring good fortune and chase away evil spirits. The Chinese believe that the longer the dragon, the more luck it will bring, and communities compete with one another to build and dance with the longest, brightest, and boldest dragon figure.

Although the bamboo dragon itself gets most of the attention during the procession, the dancers who hold up these bright, colorful spirits play a crucial role by dancing in time with the music. They put on a show themselves, while also making their dragon look like it is dancing. Those who are in front, positioning the dragon's

Revelers celebrate the New Year with the dragon dance.

head, have the greatest responsibility because the head directs the motion of the dragon. All the other dancers must keep in sync with the lead dancer's movements, or else they may trip up or disrupt the overall dance. Sometimes the lead dancer will not be carrying the dragon's head at all but will instead carry a giant pearl-like ornament, symbolizing wisdom, which the dragon chases in a spiritual quest for knowledge.

Dragon dancers primarily dance in a wavelike pattern, in time with drum music. A team that has rehearsed their movements can dance in a more complex pattern. Some run through the corkscrew patterns of the dragon, for example, whereas others make the dragon jump over obstacles. Sometimes two dragon teams will dance with each other, and on very rare occasions, nine separate dragons may share a stage, because the Chinese believe nine to be a harmonious, perfect number.

Dragon dancers prepare for a show.

Dragons in Eastern Culture

When Westerners think of dragons, they often think of fire-breathing giants that attack villages, steal treasure, guard princesses, and are defeated by valiant knights. In Eastern cultures, however, dragons symbolize great virtues, most notably intelligence, health, hard work, and good luck. These dragons can be as large as a mountain or as small as a puppy. The color of a dragon specifies its qualities as well: A green dragon reflects a good harvest, a red dragon reflects good fortune, and a gold dragon reflects prosperity. Some Eastern dragons do guard legendary treasure, but, unlike their Western counterparts, they willingly give it up to those brave and wise enough to find their hiding spots.

THAI COSTUME AND DANCE

Many cultures emphasize the importance of costumes in their dance, whether they utilize masks or shoes or dresses or jewelry. Few cultures take it to the extreme of traditional Thai dance, however, where participants will wear clothing with elaborate gold and silver crowns featuring exotic decorations ranging from bird feathers to beetle wings.

Traditional Thai dancers wear elaborate clothing and crowns during their performances.

Traditional Thai dance, called *natasin*, was meant specifically for the royal family of Thailand, and commoners did not get to enjoy such a spectacle. Though this has changed and public performances are common today, the great depth of costume design and performing movements indicate the gravity of such a dance performance. *Natasin* has its roots in the Ayutthaya period of Thai history, starting about 700 years ago, and all dances rely on 68 standardized poses and movements honed throughout the history of Thai dance.

Performers are famous for dancing along a vertical axis. Thai *natasin* dancers must keep their posture straight up and down, moving with their knees rather than extending outward with the ankles. Dancers must keep their limbs at an angle, or *wong*, at a high,

Thai dancers begin training and performing at an early age.

medium, or low level, so that their body is in a constant curve shape. Dancers are judged on how well they can maintain this *wong* throughout a performance, without slipping and changing the proportion of their stance.

Classical Thai dancers begin at an early age, usually between eight and 10. They study slow movements and fast movements that will eventually lead to their placement in the dance itself, and they learn fundamentals such as keeping the soles of their feet up and off of the ground. Students have different roles in a dance: Some are heroes, some are demons, and some are even monkeys! Those who are heroes will have the honor of wearing the most richly decorated dress during a performance, personifying the ancient pantheon of noble heroes in Thai history.

JAPAN'S *KAGURA*: FROM PRIESTS TO STAGE

The Shinto culture of ancient Japan emphasized the importance of both living and inanimate objects, from birds to stones, creating the belief that gods and spirits reside within many parts of the country. Centuries ago, Shinto priests would demonstrate the legends and myths of the faith by performing dances called *kagura*, telling the story of a god's origin or achievements in order to ask the divine for a good harvest or fishing catch. Today, Japanese *kagura* still tell these mythological stories, but the performance of these dances has been taken out of the shrines and temples and onto the main stage.

Kagura dances feature bright costumes meant to evoke the divine power of Shinto gods and exciting, dramatic movement. Dancers wear masks and wigs, and they speak in bold and powerful voices to indicate their power. Musicians playing drums, cymbals, and flutes accompany them on stage, where both music and dance are specifically timed for exact precision and consistency.

Kagura dances are performed with bright costumes, masks, and wigs.

THE *BIYELGEE*: DANCE FOR NOMADIC LIFE

Can you imagine what your life would be like if you never stayed in one place for longer than a few months? Most Mongolians are nomads, meaning that they must constantly travel with their livestock to find new pastures. Many aspects of their culture reflect this nomadic life, particularly the *biyelgee*, their traditional folk dance. Unlike other dances that take place on a large stage, *biyelgee* dancers are confined to the relatively narrow enclosure of a *ger*, a Mongolian tent-home, where they must dance in a small area, sometimes cross-legged or even sitting down.

The *biyelgee* dancers evoke traditional Mongolian nomadic life, using patterns of hand and foot movements meant to resemble the herders' life, work, and spiritual beliefs. Dancers wear bright costumes, beautiful jewelry, and artistic patterns specific to their ethnic or family group. These dances are performed among large groups during family events, weddings, and holiday celebrations. Typically, elderly Mongolians lead the dancing, while children take time to learn the steps and rhythm as they grow up and observe the dance at important events.

A Mongolian nomad wears a bright costume and beautiful jewelry during a biyelgee performance.

WAACKING ALONG IN KAZAKHSTAN

Kazakhstan is a nation of contrasts: It is the largest country in Central Asia and a leader in growth and development, although many of its people are poor and live a simple subsistence life. As Kazakhstan has tried to advance and become a modern nation, it has contributed many new artistic and cultural trends to the world, perhaps none more famous than its *waack* dance.

Waack is a modern dance, having only emerged in the 1970s, and emphasizes jerky motions of the hips and shoulders in time with a musical beat. *Waack* competitions helped the dance to spread across Central Asia, Russia, and even into Europe. Moscow's Smack and Waack competition is the largest of its kind. Kazakh dancers like Nikolai Chernikov have been ambassadors for *waack*, helping it to grow to new areas and spreading Kazakh culture along the way. The Kazakh government has not done much to support dance, meaning that individuals like Chernikov must lead the way to promote *waack*.

Waacking *competitions have helped the dance spread across Central Asia, Russia, and even Europe.*

BIG FANS OF *BUCHAECHUM*

While K-pop groups have popularized Korean music throughout the world, visitors to Korea may be much more impressed with the traditional Korean fan dance, *buchaechum*, a whirling display of color and motion. *Buchaechum* is performed by a group of female dancers, wearing the traditional *hanbok* dresses of classical Korean culture, and carrying large fans to attract the eye and whirl in time with the music. These fans are painted to resemble peony flower petals, and as a group they can create images like animals and waves.

Korean dancers perform buchaechum *at a festival.*

VIETNAM'S DANCING UNICORNS

East Asia's lion dance is derived from the Chinese dragon dance, but different cultures put different spins on these lions. In Vietnam, the dance is not a lion dance but a unicorn dance. What's more, these dancers do not work together as a group but as individuals, putting on their unicorn costume and performing solo. Performed at the Tet New Year and the autumn harvest festivals, unicorn dancers are often seen with the spirit of the earth, a large smiling man carrying a palm leaf, and their performances often more closely resemble martial arts than dance.

During the Tet New Year, the Thai people perform the lion dance as well as the unicorn dance.

Tibetan folk dancers.

KANGXIE: DANCE AT ALTITUDE

Tibet is one of the highest places on earth, famous for its location in the towering Himalaya mountains. It is also famous for being a particularly musical culture, as children learn music and dance from a very early age so they can perform during ceremonies. The *kangxie* dance is the most famous Tibetan folk dance, performed by both women and men and accompanied by musicians playing stringed instruments. Men and women dance along to the music, swaying their hands in time while singing out their love and admiration for one another.

A traditional Kandyan performance.

HEALTH AND DRUMS OF KANDYAN DANCE

The Kandy central hills of Sri Lanka have given rise to a type of dance simply known as *Kandyan*, which tells the legend of a king who suffered a great illness and was cured by three shamans who performed the dance. This dance has persisted through the centuries and is still performed today, with dancers wearing elaborate headgear, beautiful white dresses, and metallic bands that rattle as they move. It is a drumming dance that uses no other instruments to guide the motions of dancers.

CHAPTER 3 EUROPE

Although Europe is one of the smallest continents, it has a great deal of ethnic, linguistic, and cultural diversity from place to place. Some of its dance traditions can be dated back to ancient times, performed by rural peasants for centuries before being standardized by cultural authorities.

LE BALLET EN FRANÇAIS

Many cultural identities of Europe are so enmeshed with particular things—like Italian sports cars or German beer—that they are often considered one and the same. Such is often the case for the ballet, seen as a cultural icon of the French. Like some such cultural icons, however, the roots of ballet are not actually French at all. Queen Catherine de Medici imported the dance about 500 years ago from

King Louis XIV took part in the ballet in the 1600s.

Italy, taking its name from the Italian verb *ballare*, which simply means "to dance." At the time, the Italian style was quite different from modern ballet—dancers wore heavy costumes and usually performed at weddings.

In the centuries since its introduction, France has honed ballet into a symbol of the nation. Louis XIV standardized ballet during the 1600s, even dancing in ballet himself, and he created the French Académie Royale de Danse in 1661. At the time, ballet told a story, full of symbolism and myth, although all dancers playing parts were men. The first woman ballet dancer appeared in 1681. In the 1800s, the French ballet adopted the *en pointe* style of dance, in which performers stand on the very tips of their toes, moving with great grace and precision across the stage or dance floor.

Today, ballet has a wide variety of styles, ranging from classical to contemporary. Both men and women participate in this dance, which requires a great deal of physical strength and dexterity on both their parts to be able to move in sync with the music, leaping into the air (or launching their partner into the air) at a moment's notice. Modern costumes are simple and light, meant to accentuate the dancer rather than attract attention, giving them a better range of motion. Ballet is physically intense on dancers: It is common for ballet dancers to develop conditions like stress fractures, and a dancer's career is usually short because older dancers lack the strength needed to perform at a high level.

Although the ballet is graceful, it takes a toll on a dancer's body. It is common for dancers to develop conditions like stress fractures.

FLAMENCO, OLÉ!

Though almost any dance in the world evokes passion, Spain's flamenco is synonymous with intensity and desire. The flamenco has its roots in the gypsy culture of Andalusia in Southern Spain about 400 years ago. The term *flamenco* is often associated with the dance, but it actually has three separate components: dance, song, and playing of the guitar. Flamenco grew in popularity until it reached a "golden age" in the late 1800s, when it grew throughout Spain, and specific cafés, called *cafes cantantes*, sprang up to accommodate both dancers and viewers. As a result of these cafes, flamenco dance became commercialized, meaning that movements and rhythms became standardized across a nation with many cultural and linguistic differences. Famous singers and dancers like the Seville native Pepe Marchena helped to export the love of flamenco throughout the world.

Today, flamenco has become a symbol of Spanish culture. Those who wish to sing, play guitar, or dance in the flamenco take lessons from professionals, where previously any of the three needed only to jump into the fray. Flamenco

A flamenco dancer is accompanied by a percussionist and guitarist as she performs in the streets of Spain.

Flamenco puro ***performers wear frilly dresses and play castanets.***

performances fall under three categories: the *juerga*, a snap performance akin to a musical improvisation session; a professional concert where many musicians, singers, and dancers play in turn rather than featuring just one of each; and a theatrical performance where the singers, dancers, and musicians focus on technical skill rather than emotional appeal.

Flamenco puro is considered the closest type of this dance to the native gypsy performance; this is the type that has the stereotypical frilly dresses and castanets—costume pieces that are not strictly necessary for a flamenco performance. Elements of modern dance and song have led to "new flamenco," which blends together jazz elements that emphasize originality over routine.

IRISH DANCE: NO RIVER REQUIRED

Some of the oldest records of dance on the European continent come from Ireland, where Celtic druids performed ritual dances as early as 1,600 years ago in festivals celebrating natural events like solstices and eclipses. By the 1800s, Irish dance involved a dance master who would travel from village to village, performing for an audience and then moving on to the next location, famously teaching Irish children which foot was their left and which was their right. Like Irish music, Irish dance emphasized the organic and the improvisational rather than the technical. Almost all of the movement in Irish step dancing is in the lower body: The arms and torso are expected to be static so that all attention is on the movement of the feet.

Although Irish step dancing is about 200 years old, the theatrical show popularly known as *Riverdance* is much more recent, having only been developed in 1995 for a televised dance competition. Nevertheless, this style has taken both Ireland and the world by storm, with ensemble dance troupes performing *Riverdance* to sold-out venues.

Riverdance is a dance ensemble that travels and performs to sold-out venues.

THE *POLSKA*—OF SWEDEN, NOT POLAND

Although the name "*polska*" might make you think about Poland, it is a dance that originated in Scandinavia, not Poland—although the name is thought to be taken from a Polish nobility dance from about 500 years ago. The *polska* has evolved from one specific meaning to many, and in some Scandinavian nations it simply means a dance that is in 3/4 time with no other specific standards. Usually the first and third beats involve movement or kicking, while the second beat in the musical structure is a pause. It is a couples' dance, meant for two people who grasp each other firmly as they pivot in smooth coordination around a central step.

The *polska* is considered the oldest dance in Sweden. There are two specific steps in the Swedish version: The first has each member of the couple turn behind the other in a counterclockwise trajectory, whereas the second has the couple place their feet in between each other to be able to step backward in alternating directions. As a result, many newcomers often trip over themselves while trying to dance the *polska*!

Polska *couples touch hands as they pivot around a central step.*

BOHEMIA'S TRADITION OF POLKA

According to tradition, a Czech peasant girl named Anna Slezak invented the polka, for no other reason than she enjoyed it, one step at a time. The word *polka* itself is derived from a Czech term meaning "half-step," which is why the dance itself involves participants lightly going from foot to foot with grace and timing. Polka exploded onto the European dance scene in the 1800s, becoming popular throughout major cities and spreading into new places like the United States as immigrant communities expanded overseas.

The sound of polka music is quite unique and instantly recognizable: the accordion provides the 2/4 timing while pairs of dancers go from half-steps to hops to full sweeps. One of the reasons why polka became so popular is because dancers can go in whatever direction they choose. But not being bound by lines or angles means that dancers on a polka floor must pay close attention so they don't become entangled with other dancing pairs.

Czech dancers perform the polka.

RANCHOS ENERGETICOS

Men and women pause during the ranchos *to snap their fingers.*

The national folk dance of Portugal is called *ranchos*, one of several folk dances that stems from peasant culture and is most often associated with weddings and holidays. This partner dance involves very colorful clothing: full-length dresses for women and trousers and vests for men. Each community in Portugal puts its own spin on the *ranchos*, but most feature a line or circle dance, where participants will pause on downbeats to snap their fingers, changing partners as they go. High-speed spinning can make both participants and viewers alike grow dizzy. Guitars, accordions, and even bagpipes provide the musical accompaniment.

THE TARANTELLA: BEWARE THE BITE

Legend in Italy holds that a tarantula spider will cause a person to go into a feverish trance that can be cured only by intensive dance. This dance, in turn, is called the *tarantella*, and it is as intense a dance as you'll find. It's a courtship dance, meant to be performed between male and female partners, where each one teases and flirts with the other through gestures, twirls, and expression. It is a mainstay at Sicilian weddings, where the bride and groom dance to the music of tambourines and a wooden flute called a *friscalettu*, decorated with colored ribbons.

When a large group dances the tarantella, they will join hands and form a circle. At times, the group will make its way in and out of the center of the circle.

MIRRORING YOUR PARTNER IN THE CZARDAS

Men and women mirror one another when dancing the czardas.

Some partner dances require a great deal of synchronization to avoid falling over one another. Among the Jewish cultures of Eastern Europe, however, mirror dances like the *czardas* take this a step further by requiring that both participants (usually a man leading a woman) mirror each other's moves precisely: The man starts on his right foot, and the woman on her left. They dance on the downbeat and pause on the upbeat. Traditional Hasidic Jewish communities do not approve of mixed-gender dances, although the majority of modern Eastern European Jews no longer enforce these strict norms.

KICK THE HAT IN NORWAY

In the Norwegian folk dance, halling, *a dancer must literally kick the hat off of a stick.*

The Norwegian folk dance known as *halling* is perhaps the oldest folk dance in Northern Europe. Like other folk dances, it originated in the peasant community and is a mainstay at weddings. Unlike other folk dances, it is a solo feature, where a dancer must keep time with a violinist. It is most famous for the climax of the dance: A girl will hold a hat up on a stick, and the dancer must leap into the air and kick the hat off of the stick. This part of the dance, called *kast*, is considered a feat of strength, because the hat may be as high as 9 feet (3 meters) up off the ground.

CHAPTER 4 LATIN AMERICA AND THE CARIBBEAN

To some, the term "Latin America" itself evokes ideas of dance, whether fiery and up-tempo or slow and methodical. Latin American culture is synonymous with *machismo*, and the majority of dances are meant for two partners, a dominant male and a following female.

BRAZIL'S IDENTITY: SOCCER AND SAMBA

Along with rain forests and soccer, the samba dances of Brazil form a major aspect of the national identity. Samba's history dates back over 300 years, back to the time when Brazil's population was a mix of white colonists, native populations, and black slaves. Much of samba derives primarily from the latter category, and the name itself hails from an Angolan word meaning "an invitation to dance," while elements of the dance can be traced to rhythms from Western Africa. Slave markets in Brazil are thought to be the original point for samba dancing; this was a place where blacks met and performed ritual dances as part of religious expression.

Samba has much more than just one cultural component, however. The zesty musical accompaniment is a result of cultural influences from Spain to the United States, as guitar and percussion instruments play a major role in keeping time and changing rhythms. Immigrants from European nations like Germany added elements from polka dancing. Finally, the omnipresence of the Catholic Church in Brazil has meant that samba was integrated into a number of religious festivals and holidays, most notably Carnival, the world-famous celebration that takes place just prior to Lent.

Samba itself is a very rapid dance whose frantic movement of all limbs, suggestive shaking of body parts, and up-tempo beats require the dancer to be in good shape. There are official dance steps, but participants have the freedom to choose their own moves and routine in order to show

Guitarists and percussionists gather to provide the changing rhythms of samba.

Samba schools and dancers from various cities compete annually at the Carnival celebration. São Paulo holds the second largest Carnival celebration in Brazil.

choose their own moves and routine in order to show off to a crowd or just a single viewer. Elaborate costumes, including many that reveal quite a bit of skin, are not just common but encouraged. During the Carnival celebration, an entire street may turn into a giant samba dance, without any rules except to maintain time with the beat of the music.

Brazil's Carnival

Called the world's biggest party, Carnival is the celebration of the final days of the calendar prior to the Christian holiday of Lent, the weeks leading up until Easter, when adherents must deny themselves particular comforts, from meat to chocolate to alcohol. Carnival, as such, is the celebration of all the good things in life that will be off limits as soon as Lent comes. Each year, the Brazilian city of Rio de Janeiro plays host to the largest Carnival celebration, with over a million tourists coming each year to enjoy the good times—while they still last.

IT TAKES TWO TO TANGO

Where Brazil is world-renowned for samba, next-door neighbor Argentina is synonymous with the tango. Tango is a partner dance that originated in the capital city, Buenos Aires, in the 1700s; it too blends elements of different ethnic and social groups to make a dance that appeals to all members of the population. The first tango dancers were slaves who met up at various locations. In the late 1700s, the government banned these tangos for fear that slave meetings could lead to rebellions. Not until 100 years later did the tango reappear and take Argentina (and later the world) by storm.

Tangos became popular in the late 1800s, when bar owners would employ bands of musicians to attract patrons. These musicians played to the crowd, who wanted a faster partner dance, usually to woo women. As this music became mainstream, more and more Argentinians wanted to dance to it. And when Argentinian bands toured through Europe and the United States, people there also developed a taste for it in turn. This led to an

A couple dances the tango on the streets of Buenos Aires.

One of the most important directions a partner will give in the tango is the dip.

internationalization of tango and a wide variety of evolutions of the form, with differences in many nations today.

The modern tango is a partner dance that uses a lead-and-follow direction: One partner (usually, but not necessarily, the man) will direct the other around the dance floor, indicating when to turn, when to twirl, and, most importantly, when to dip. Dancers are intimate, embracing each other shoulder to shoulder and chest to chest, and they frequently employ complex footwork and choreography to wow onlookers. There are many varieties of tango, as more and more types of music are applied to the dance. Ballroom tango, for example, takes a slower and more methodical pace, while hip-hop tango has dancers moving along to a rap beat rather than a traditional orchestra.

THE SALSA OF CUBA

Cuba is the origin of world-famous salsa dancing, but this style of dance is unusual in that its roots are far more modern than many other Latin American dances. In the 1950s, prior to the Communist revolution, social clubs and bars would organize large group dances that became known as *salsa*, with people moving about in a large circle called *rueda*. Cubans quickly developed a taste for the dance, which persevered through revolution and depression to become a national cultural marker. It too was exported around the world, and different nations have put their own spin on salsa dancing. The music that accompanies salsa, called *sabor*, is renowned for its fast beat and loud volume.

Cuban salsa dancing is particularly demanding on the dancers. The motion is meant to be continual, with no breaks in the action to catch your breath. Partners twirl one another around in a giant unending *rueda*, where dance is both

***Musicians offer music that is called* sabor.**

Salsa dancers are surrounded by musicians in their **rueda**.

improvised and synchronized so that individual partners can strut their stuff—but they must finish in time with everyone else. Like other Latin American dances, the partners are usually male and female, and the male is expected to lead, putting his foot either in front of or behind the beat, with the female following in time. Footwork is crucial to salsa dancing, and those who cannot keep up will quickly become tangled.

Salsa dancing has evolved into quite a few forms around the globe. One interesting form is called *suelto*, which involves dancing without another partner at all; instead, an individual performs in front of an orchestra or band before a crowd. Another, called *trios*, has two leads who share a follow, passing the partner about in an elaborate choreography to demonstrate mastery of form and the ability to move in and out of another partner's synchronized dance.

PLAINS DANCING: *JOROPO*

Both Columbia and Venezuela in South America have similar geographic patterns: About half of each country is hilly, while half is lowland. The plains and the mountains each have their distinct cultures shared across geographical borders. In both nations, the plains culture dances to *joropo*, associated with the ranching flavor of the countryside. *Joropo* requires an entire string ensemble to create the music—rather than relying on sets of drums for the beat, instruments like guitars and upright bass provide the percussion as well as the melody. At the center of the music and the dance is the harp, the iconic instrument of South American plains cowboys.

Joropo is divided into slow (*pasajes*) and fast (*golpes*) dances. In both cases, dancers will use hand turns and waltz turns to move their partners about, holding them tightly and performing sweeping movements before separating to dance backward and forward. Men stomp their feet in time with the music while women sweep over the dance floor before the two partners return to each other.

***Partners take part in dancing the* joropo.**

CUECA, CHILE, AND CHICKENS

The national dance of Chile, the *cueca*, is compared to the courting ritual of a rooster and a chicken, as partners in a dance will circle about each other without ever touching, exaggerating their movements and their gestures in time with the music. Unlike many other Latin American dances, whose histories are quite well established, it is not clear when or where the *cueca* first originated. What is clear is that it became popular as a courtship dance among all classes of Chilean society.

Participants wear the traditional Chilean dress while dancing: Men wear hats, ponchos, and riding boots, and women wear flowery dresses. Participants begin with the man offering his arm to the woman; they then proceed to the dance floor and pull out white handkerchiefs. Holding these handkerchiefs in the air, the two partners dance while waving the cloths, never touching one another but dancing in and out. The male is expected to be aggressive, whereas the woman is reserved. The dance ends with the man on one knee and the woman placing a foot on his other knee.

Chilean cueca dancers wear traditional dress when performing.

FROM A TO ZAMACUECA IN PERU

The legacy of Spain's empire throughout Latin America can be reflected in many cultural aspects, including dance. The Peruvian *zamacueca* is one such legacy, beginning when Peru was a viceroyalty of Spain rather than an independent nation. The *zamacueca* blends together Spanish, native Indian, and black slave cultures to create a totally new type of movement. European stringed instruments such as the guitar and the harp provide the music behind the *zamacueca*, and an Andean wooden box called a *cajon* gives the percussion needed for a consistent beat. The song of a *zamacueca* is a sad one, a melody in a minor mode, and the dance follows this emotion in slow, precise movements.

Zamacueca reached its peak popularity centuries ago, when Peru was perhaps the most important of the South American colonies. It evolved to become a dance celebrating liberation from Spain in the 1800s, but it faded in popularity after that. Today, it is no longer performed except as an exhibition, although some Peruvian dance institutions teach the *zamacueca* to students.

This dance company performs the zamacueca at a fair in Lima, Peru.

COMPAS AND VODOU

A traditional vodou ritual.

Any mention of Haitian culture must mention vodou, more commonly called voodoo—the spiritual beliefs and practices that dominate the island. Haiti's most popular dance, called *compas*, can be a part of a vodou ritual meant to cleanse the mind or soul, but it can also be performed on its own as a celebration. *Compas* has sometimes been called the salsa of Haiti, and similarities include a quick tempo, musical accompaniment by guitars, and the ability to dance solo. *Compas* emphasizes the movement of particular body parts that salsa does not, however, including the shoulders, arms, hips, and feet. What's more, saxophone and keyboard are common instruments to provide a beat.

REGGAE AND DANCE

Jamaican dancers dance the kumina.

The island of Jamaica produced reggae culture, and although reggae is more commonly associated with music than dance, the *kumina* reggae dance shows off the vitality of the island. While *kumina* is performed at funerals and wakes, it is the farthest thing in the world from a sad dance. Participants are in constant movement, with upper body and arms as well as pelvic isolations moving in time with the drumbeat. *Kumina* draws on the history of African culture that dominates Jamaica, as dancers perform to call to the spirits of ancestors and provide relief to those who knew the deceased. A tradition called Nine Nights has friends and family dance the *kumina* for nine days as the burial is prepared and carried out.

MAKING MERENGUE IN THE DOMINICAN REPUBLIC

Merengue can be described as a dance, but it is so much more to the peoples of the Dominican Republic. The word can be a festival, a type of music, or even a way of life. Merengue festivals take place throughout the Dominican Republic in both big cities and small villages. Dancers circle their partners in pairs, using flirtatious gestures to get attention and show off. Instruments like the accordion and the saxophone keep the beat, and young children learn how to dance the merengue at an early age. The dance crosses many social boundaries that are otherwise guarded in the country, allowing participants to shed their status for a good time.

A couple flirtatiously dances the merengue.

Street performers dance the beguine.

BIG BEGUINE BALLS

The small Caribbean island of Martinique, like many others, fused white European culture with black African culture during the colonial period. Martinique developed a number of cultural legacies from this synthesis, and its most famous musical product was the beguine, a type of dancing that is both quite formal and quite relaxed and can be enjoyed in both a ballroom setting and with a simple *bélé* drum. The contrast has led to different names: beguine *de salon* and beguine *de rue* mean a dance meant to be performed at a ballroom and on the street, respectively. The dance can be slow or up-tempo, as desired, and can be performed in a group or with a single partner.

CHAPTER 5 MIDDLE EAST

From Morocco to Pakistan, the Middle East represents something of a paradox for dance. Some ultra-orthodox Islamic governments totally outlaw dance, whereas others encourage dance types that have existed for centuries. In some parts of the Middle East, furthermore, ultramodern skyscrapers play host to dance clubs playing today's top hits.

THE SAUDI SWORD DANCE

Saudi Arabia puts on a national festival each year to celebrate its culture and heritage. One of the headline events of the festival is the *ardha*, or sword dance, which is without a doubt one of the most unique dances in the entire world. The *ardha* pays homage to the Bedouin (nomad) history of the Saudi nation, drawing upon centuries during which Saudi Arabians had little more than their horses, their flocks, and their swords to call their own. The Saudi cultural authorities say that this dance reflects the national strength and character, whereas the weapons themselves symbolize pride and independence. The name itself comes from a term meaning "to show," and it references a time when participants in combat would draw themselves up before the enemy to intimidate their foes prior to fighting.

This particular dance is male-only. Rows of men line up across from one another, carrying a sword or a cane or a similar object. They wear traditional clothing: a long coat with a tailored cut of triangular sleeves meant to symbolize the robes worn by nomads for protection against the sun and sand. Participants

Men line up and perform the* ardha *accompanied by a percussionist.

***Dressed in traditional clothing, Saudi men line up, carrying a sword to perform the* ardha.**

stand shoulder to shoulder as music and drums establish a tempo, while a performer speaks traditional poetry. Dancers move their feet in time with the music while waving their swords forward and backward. There is no exact footwork required, provided that all participants move in time and sync with one another.

Today, the sword dance is usually performed only at the most important occasions and celebrations. It has gained notoriety for its performances in front of visiting dignitaries and heads of state, meant to impress them with a vigorous display of Saudi culture and history.

THE EVOLUTION OF ISRAELI DANCE

Israel is one of the newest nations in the world, having been established only in 1948. Prior to this, however, questions and debate about creating a Jewish homeland—a philosophy called Zionism—dated back centuries. At the same time that Zionists debated the creation of a Jewish nation, they also debated the composition of Jewish culture, including music and dance. With a wide range of Jews living throughout the global diaspora, from Europe to Central Asia, what aspects of culture should be included in a new national identity?

Jewish folk dance proved to be an integral part of the development of Israeli culture. An Israeli politician named Gurit Kadman said that for Israeli Jews who "fervently" wished to have dances of their own, it was necessary to create a new

At the end of Passover, revelers gather to sing and dance.

The Karmiel Dance Company of Israel performs in South Korea.

synthesis of dance from existing folk dances. Early folk dances had names like "Water, Water" and "The Pomegranate Tree," reflecting both the difficulties and successes of creating a new life in a desert environment. These dances were meant for Jewish high holidays and community performances.

Newer folk dances in Israel today have totally shed the previous references to deserts, shepherds, and the Bible. Instead, they import pop music from throughout the Mediterranean, borrowing from Turkish, Greek, and Arabic dance trends to create a completely new identity and thus changing the definition of Jewish identity by melding it with other cultures and concepts. There are some 3,000 Israeli folk dances today, from the traditional to the hypermodern. As one example, the traditional Yemenite step dance involves moving to the beat one note at a time, for hours on end, with the entire community in sync. By contrast, the Karmiel Dance Festival celebrates new types of dance, melding folk dance with worldwide trends, and attracting visitors from across the world to see the newest moves.

CAN YOU STOMACH THE BELLY DANCE?

Ancient Egyptian hieroglyphs depict dancers at festivals thousands of years old, perhaps depicting the first standardized dance in all of human history. Fast-forward through the centuries, and the Egyptian people have not lost their love of a catchy beat. Their most famous dance, known simply as the belly dance, has spread like wildfire due to its complex movements and tantalizing gestures.

Known in Arabic simply as "Arabic dance," the belly dance originated in Egypt centuries ago. Ancient writers describe Egyptian dancers performing in much the same way as modern belly dancers—sinking to the floor on their knees, clicking castanets, and undulating their torsos in a provocative fashion. Travelers through

A belly dancer sinks to the floor, often clicking castanets and undulating their torso in a provocative fashion.

Belly dancing is still a form of entertainment for travelers who come to Egypt.

the centuries who came to see Egyptian pyramids commented on these dances and mentioned their unique appeal.

The belly dance, as the name suggests, requires a great deal of stomach muscle to pull off. It is typically a solo dance, meant for exhibition and public performance, where a dancer (almost always a woman) will move her stomach in time with the music. She wears minimal clothing to show off her stomach, legs, and arms, adding a particularly sensual element to the dance. Fluid, continuous motion is a hallmark of the belly dance, with the performer moving horizontally and vertically as she chooses, relying on organic movement rather than conforming to choreographed steps. Hips and shoulders propel the dancer forward, backward, and to the side at the same time that she shakes and shimmies.

The music of belly dancing is typically very simple. It may be as little as a single person on a drum or tambourine keeping time, while a more complex or public performance might feature an entire band. New Age Arabic techno music complements the motion of belly dancers just as well as traditional Egyptian music played on instruments like the *oud* lute or the *quan* strings.

DOING THE *DABKE*

The area of the Eastern Mediterranean known as the Levant has a great deal of overlapping cultures between nations like Lebanon, Syria, and Jordan. One shared aspect of culture in the Levant is the Arabic folk dance known as the *dabke*, a group dance popular at weddings, festivals, holidays, and other important occasions. A *dabke* fuses together line dancing and circle dancing, with participants standing in a line with a leader on one side. This leader must provide the basic flow of the dance, which alternates direction as it goes.

The term *dabke* simply means "stamping the feet," and some historians suggest that it has roots in an ancient planting ritual in which farmers would jump on the ground to frighten away evil spirits from their crops. Whatever the origin, *dabke* has evolved into different forms throughout the Arabic nations of the Levant, some men-only and some women-only, but most feature a lead dancer breaking away from the group to improvise a unique dance to the beat before returning to the line.

Dancers perform the* dabke *on stage at a festival.

PERFECT PERSIAN DANCE

Persian dance has a history as old as Persia itself, dating back thousands of years and kept alive to this day in Iran, neighboring nations with Persian populations, and throughout the Persian diaspora. Like many other Middle Eastern dances, the motion is meant to be fluid, with adherence to the beat but not a strict choreography that must be followed closely. The aesthetic of a body line means that Persian dance emphasizes the motion of the wrists, the coordination of both arms and legs, and the foot patterns used by dancers.

The ancient art of Persian dance is kept alive in Iran, neighboring nations with Persian populations, and people of Persian descent living around the world.

Hands are usually considered the most important part of many Persian dances. The hands must flow as the body flows, directing movement and channeling energy through the arms to the fingertips. It is important in many Persian dances to extend the fingers: The *abshar*, or waterfall, is a dance motion that involves extending fingers outward as both hands pull away from one another, creating a symmetrical motion.

Dance and the Law in Iran

The Islamic Republic of Iran is famously one of the most repressive societies in the world today, governed by strict Islamic principles that restrict the population from many freedoms enjoyed in Western nations. Dance is one such restriction, because Iran has many laws that require public "modesty," especially for women. Dancing in public can be seen as indecent, whereas any dress that reveals a woman's body is considered *haram*, or strictly forbidden. Public dance performances may involve only men. Despite some liberalization of Iran's strict religious laws, the government remains particularly uncompromising about basic aspects of everyday life. One of the most publicized Iranian restrictions on the rights of women is the law forcing women to wear a hijab, or head covering, in public.

AFGHANISTAN AND THE ATTAN

As in many other Middle Eastern nations, Afghani folk dance dates back centuries, and many aspects of the origin of its folk dances remain shrouded in mystery and speculation. The most popular dance in Afghanistan, the *attan*, features large groups of dancers, usually 10 or more, at weddings and other ceremonies. A large drum called a *dhol* keeps the beat for participants, while a *sorna* pipe provides the melody. *Attan* dancers slowly circle about the drummer, whose pace increases faster and faster. Dancers are encouraged to perform as they see fit, sometimes singing along, sometimes snapping fingers, sometimes clapping to the beat.

Attan dancers carry handkerchiefs that they pull out and twirl about during a song. They whirl their body about, causing the handkerchief to fly about in turn. Although most *attan* dancers are men, they may include women in the performance and sing or recite poetry to them, while the women dance with scarves in their hands.

The large drum called a* dhol*, keeps beat for the dancers.

AL-BAR'AH: THE DAGGER DANCE

The small nation of Oman in the Southern Arabian Peninsula shares many things with its northern neighbor, Saudi Arabia. One interesting overlap is their weapon dances, but though Saudis have a sword dance, the Omanis have a dagger dance. The *Al-Bar'ah* is a warrior dance in which a circle of men and women play drums and flutes. Two dancers stand up with daggers in hand, thrusting them backward and forward in time with the music; although the steps are not difficult, the coordination is challenging. Each tribe of Oman has its own take on *Al-Bar'ah*, typically performed outdoors during celebrations.

Traditionally, the Al-Bar'ah *is performed with daggers, but each Omani tribe has its own take on the dance.*

CHOBI, AN ASSYRIAN CIRCLE

Although Arabs account for the majority of the population of the Middle East, the Assyrian population of Syria and next-door Iraq has a distinct ethnicity and culture separate from the Arab majority. One of the differences between the two is the Assyrian circle dance, *chobi*, which is popular in Iraq. Participants in this folk dance form a circle and kick their feet forward and back at the same time that they wave their arms forward and back, creating a dynamic where they must keep their balance as they sway to the beat. *Chobi* is common at Assyrian weddings, where the bride and groom demonstrate their ability to dance.

Men and women dance the chobi *at a wedding.*

MODERN DANCE OF THE GULF: *KHALEEGI*

Arab girls dancing the **khaleegi**.

The word *khaleegi* simply means "gulf," and this dance is broadly performed throughout the Arabic world, most notably at weddings, where a participant may start by herself but soon is joined by a throng of dancers. It is usually a female dance, and *khaleegi* requires a specific outfit, namely, a two-piece dress meant to display feminine physical traits. Dancers attempt to recreate the image of a sea wave moving as they move their heads, hands, and hips along in time to the music. One particular aspect that makes *khaleegi* unique is that dancers shake their hair from side to side as they go, making their hair part of the dance, along with their other body parts.

Dancers hold hands and create a large circle when dancing the Kurdish **halparke**.

HALPARKE: MAKING A KURDISH CIRCLE

The Kurdish circle dance known as *halparke* reflects the minority status of the Kurd ethnic group in the Middle East, commenting on a long history of struggle and strife to be accepted and find a home. Dancers hold hands with each other in a large circle, with one dancer at the head holding a particularly important item, like a relic or a book. This leader performs the dance, taking the group in a circle, before stepping back and allowing another to take the leader spot. This Kurdish dance is famously fast, requiring all participants to be able to match the leader's motions at a rapid clip.

CHAPTER 6 NORTH AMERICA

Because the United States is a global exporter of culture and music, many of its dance types have become world famous. Nevertheless, North America includes Canada and Mexico, which have also contributed unique dances to the world stage.

BREAK A LEG

Breakdancing represents one of the most dynamic forms of dance on the entire planet, requiring individuals to contort and spin their bodies in ways that require tremendous practice to master. Breakdancing is unique in that it is almost entirely improvisational, lacking any standardized choreography or formal moves. Though you may think that the term *breakdancing* refers to the likelihood that the dancers will break a bone as they dance, it actually refers to the mixing of different songs and sounds together by DJs to produce continuous music and continuous motion by dancers.

Breakdancing began in the 1970s, when American dance clubs engaged in battles in which participants had to come up with increasingly complex moves, forcing opponents to either mimic the movement or develop a more complex dance move themselves. Hip-hop pioneers popularized breakdancing, most notably the New York DJ

Breakdancing is a popular form of street performing, especially in large cities. When you see a crowd, there will often be a dancer or troupe of dancers performing.

Freezes come in all shapes.

notably the New York DJ Kool Herc, and it then spread out from New York and into new areas of the country and the world. Though originally considered an African American male dance, it quickly crossed racial and gender barriers to become an instant sensation, with many nations across the world developing their own particular style unique to their cultures.

In general, breakdancing is characterized by four particular movements. *Toprock* refers to any steps that are performed while standing, often opening up a dance competition, whereas *downrock* refers to movements on the floor, where dancers rely on their hands as much as their feet. *Power moves* require a greater deal of strength and stamina, including spinning around on one's head. Finally, *freezes* are moves that require the dancer to become totally still, emphasizing body control, strength, and timing. Breakdancing involves adherence to a beat, usually hip-hop, but there is no defined music accompaniment, and some break-dancers will use country or classical music to demonstrate their abilities.

DON'T BE A SQUARE

Considered one of the most iconic American dances in history, square dancing reflects American culture itself by drawing on a huge variety of different influences, ranging from European folk dances to African step dances. Named the official folk dance of 31 different states, square dancing, famous for its slow pace and communal nature, is more commonly associated with the Western and Southern states. Though it's considered a dance of white Americans, it has many different cultural roots, including the historical use of blacks as "callers" who added their own interpretation to the movements.

A typical square dance features four partners (eight dancers in total), who move around the open space of a square pattern. Unlike dances that demand originality, square dancing is completely choreographed and requires that all participants follow the same foot movements to successfully go from start to finish. However, the choreography depends on the caller, meaning that no two square

Square dancing requires four partners—eight dancers in total.

Square dance partners enjoy the calls made by the caller.

dances are the same and that there can be a great deal of difference between each moves in a set. All dancers begin in the square, following steps that are spoken out loud by the caller; there may be as few as four steps or as many as several dozen. It's not always easy to follow the caller, so many square dancers enjoy recovering from failure just as much as succeeding, because mistakes are part of the entertainment.

Square dance music is primarily country music, played with guitars, fiddles, banjos, and double bass. The music is not normally fast, although a band can play an up-tempo piece to accelerate the dance when desired. Square dance clubs may change up the dance altogether by having participants dance to hip-hop or techno instead of country music, making them concentrate in an entirely new way.

SWING ALONG TO SWING DANCE

The development of swing dancing is closely tied to the development of jazz music from the 1920s to the 1940s, a time of great change in America, when factors like Prohibition and the Great Depression raised questions about what it meant to be an American. Swing dancing was part of this cultural trend, shedding the conservative dance patterns of yesteryear to embrace new, dynamic, fast-paced dance in time with jazz music. The speed of the dance, as well as its association with the African American community, made many traditional white communities skeptical about swing, and many banned it altogether.

Different swing dances emerged in the period of the 1920s remembered as the Roaring Twenties, a time of economic growth and challenges to social norms. Some of the most famous swing dances, like the Jitterbug or the Charleston, still

Many swing dancers are still inspired by the 1920s. They incorporate the style and the fashion of the era into their performances.

remain, practiced by professional and amateur dancers alike. Others, like the Balboa, have not fared as well and are usually displayed only as exhibitions. Swing dancing is generally considered to have originated in African American communities, primarily Harlem in New York City, at the same time that jazz music became mainstream. Swing dancing evolved on separate coasts: East Coast Swing and West Coast Swing have different beats and foot styles, even if they look and sound similar to a viewer.

Swing dancing is often a social event, held in parks and dance studios.

Swing dancing, in general, can be done in a tight area, because partners hold on to each other's hands without moving very far away from their starting position. One partner (usually male) tends to lead, twirling the other about and leading with footsteps and shoulder position. Swing dancing is famous for its vertical motion: Participants can lift each other up, or even throw each other into the air, at the climax of a beat. However, other swing dances emphasize fast movement rather than dramatic movement, requiring both participants to shift and spin constantly as they move forward and backward.

The Harlem Renaissance

The neighborhood of Harlem in New York City has been a key component of African American culture for much of U.S. history but particularly during the 1920s to the 1940s, a period of time remembered as the Harlem Renaissance. A wide variety of artists, thinkers, writers, and musicians lived in Harlem at this time, ranging from the jazz musician Duke Ellington to the politician and orator Marcus Garvey. The leaders of the Harlem Renaissance helped to push the culture of African Americans into the greater mainstream, and they had a key role in the ultimate development of the civil rights movement of the 1950s and 1960s.

HATS OFF IN MEXICO

Perhaps the most common dance of Mexico is known as *jarabe tapatío*, the "hat dance," and the sombreros worn by the male dancers leave no question about how the dance got its name. *Jarabe tapatío* is a partner dance performed by groups that range in size from just a pair to many pairs in sync. A courtship dance, both participants in the *jarabe tapatío* are dressed to the nines: Men wear a suit, whereas women wear the flowing *poblano* dresses famous to Mexico.

As is common to Hispanic courtship dances, neither participant touches the other but instead maintains a discreet distance. Men dance with their hands behind their backs, and women twirl the hems of their dresses in wide circles to create a flowing pattern. The partner dance becomes a line dance as the beat changes, with the men and women moving to separate sides and then dancing in line past one another. Usually a single pair will come to the forefront of the dance floor or stage to demonstrate their skill and elaborate footwork.

***Dancers perform the* jarabe tapatío.**

DANCING FOR RAIN

Although countless types of Native American dances have been performed for centuries, the most well known are the rain dances performed by a wide number of cultures throughout the Western and Southwestern United States. The rain dance, as the name suggests, invokes the spirits of the weather and the sky to send rain to the parched deserts and prairies so that crops like corn can grow. Typically, this dance occurs prior to the planting season, though it is also performed in times of great drought.

The rain dance is a unique Native American dance in that both men and women participate—a contrast to warrior dances, where only men are allowed to perform. Each dance varies from tribe to tribe: Some wear elaborate masks and headdresses with hundreds of brightly colored feathers, whereas others don animal skins to mimic the beasts they share the land with. One constant is the color blue, usually in the form of bird feathers and turquoise jewelry, which symbolizes both water and wind. Most rain dances are performed in a zigzag motion rather than standing in a circle.

This Native American tribe performs its rain dance with brightly colored bird feathers.

THE MOSH PIT: DOWN AND DIRTY

A number of popular music genres, most notably metal and punk, drive listeners into such a frenzy that they have to dance to release their energy. At concerts throughout North America, this takes on a unique form: the mosh pit. A mosh pit can just as accurately be called dancing as it can be called a brawl, a no-holds-barred contest where participants throw themselves at one another in appreciation of their favorite band. Injuries, both minor and major, are typical in mosh pits.

Despite the seeming brutality, a mosh pit actually involves several dance techniques. One is called skanking, where participants run and thrust their arms at the same time, sometimes forward and sometimes backward. Wrecking involves two participants hitting each other in the chest, as hard or as soft as they desire. Where a mosh pit also has a fire pit, participants will one-up each other by leaping over the flames, doing their best to avoid getting burned.

Mosh pits often look like concertgoers are violently brawling with one another.

DRUMS OF THE NORTH

Inuit drum dances have been going on for hundreds of years.

The Inuit people of Northern Canada and Alaska have few resources with which to make instruments. As a result, their primary instruments are drums made of animal skin stretched over bone or wood. Men compose drum dance songs, or *pisiit*, while they are out hunting, and the topic of the song is often hunting itself. When they return home, they teach the song to their wives, who in turn teach it to other women in the Inuit community. Members dance to the beat of the song and the drums, in igloos of ice large enough to hold as many as 100 members of the tribe.

CLOGGING: HEEL TO TOE

Cloggers participate in a local parade wearing their wooden shoes.

There's not much reason to wear a clog out and about, because the wooden shoes are famously hard and inflexible. However, they make an excellent sound when struck on a dance floor, which has led to clog dancing, or "clogging." Popular in the Appalachian Mountain range of the Eastern United States, clog dancing resembles tap dancing but with a much heavier beat. These Appalachian communities developed the dance from their ancestors, who came across the Atlantic Ocean from the Netherlands, Germany, and Sweden, where clogs were easy and affordable to make compared to leather shoes. Dancers can clog along to a bluegrass band or simply make their own beat as they go.

SNAKE GOT YOUR TONGUE?

The Snake Dance photographed in 1889.

One of the most widely publicized Native American dances throughout the United States since the time of contact in the 1800s was the Hopi Snake Dance, so named because Hopi tribal dancers would literally place live snakes in their mouths while dancing. Believed to be a type of water dance, because snakes were associated with springs and guardianship of water, the Hopi gathered snakes for two weeks prior to the dance and had them watched over to prevent escape. A priest would lightly stroke the snakes with a feather to attune them to human presence, and then dancers would put them in their mouths and dance. After the ceremony ended, the snakes were released to the four points of the compass to take the prayers of the Hopi people out to the world.

A young girl learns the cha-cha-chá dance.

GOT RHYTHM? DANCE THE CHA-CHA-CHÁ

The Cuban community of the United States has spread its influence over much of the country, although most of the population has settled in Florida. One major aspect of Cuban American culture is the cha-cha-chá dance, so named because three standard beats make the participants dance on the floor in a one-two-three fashion before the tempo increases (though it is often called the "cha-cha" in the United States). With a melody that is strongly connected to the downbeat, the cha-cha-chá is one of the easiest North American dances to learn, because participants usually need only follow the rhythm of the song as they go.

CHAPTER 7 OCEANIA

The island cultures from Indonesia to Easter Island are united by musical traditions. The progression of song and dance over the centuries has created a number of rhythms and movements found nowhere else in the world, some modern and some ancient.

BEDHAYA: DANCING FOR THE SULTAN

The island of Java in Indonesia has a tradition of dance that dates back centuries and reflects the wide variety of influences that have taken hold on the big isle throughout history. The most important of them all is the *bedhaya*, the sacred Javanese court dance, which has symbolic and religious meaning. Performed by nine dancers at the most important events of the ancient kingdom, such as a coronation or a sultan's birthday, *bedhaya* dates back at least 400 years to a religious ceremony that wed the Sultan Senapati to the mythical Queen of the Southern Sea. *Bedhaya* today is exhibitionist rather than ceremonial, because sultans no longer rule Indonesia.

The *bedhaya* dance is very slow and deliberate. Dancers appear on stage in sarong dresses, walking in an arranged pattern as they enter and kneel down in respect prior to starting the dance itself. The footwork of the dance itself is not complicated, but each participant weaves in and out of the group in a pattern akin to moving pieces on a chessboard. Interestingly,

The* bedhaya *dance begins with dancers kneeling. Their footwork is slow and deliberate as they dance.

Bedhaya *dancers wear sarong dresses for their performance.*

the expression on the faces of these dancers is always neutral, without emotion or range, never even lifting their eyes up to look at the audience. Though a variety of hand gestures are used in *bedhaya*, they have no specific meaning other than to streamline the movement itself. Likewise, a chorus of singers provides a melody, typically sad and spiritual, but the words of the melody themselves have no meaning and instead only convey emotion.

Bedhaya dancers begin in a squatting position, making it physically challenging to dance. They weave throughout their group, bending in time with the dance, and all but two main dancers will slowly leave in the same pattern as they arrived. The final two dancers engage in a battlelike display using a pair of daggers called a *kriss*, mimicking combat.

DANCING DOWN UNDER

The island of Australia has become a melting pot of various different cultures over the centuries, as Aboriginal peoples came into contact first with European colonists and then with East Asian immigrants. Australians today try to preserve Aboriginal culture to prevent total assimilation, which may result in traditional songs and dances being lost forever. Institutions like the Bangarra Dance Theater attempt to keep Aboriginal dances alive and display them to the public so that they will not be forgotten.

There are many different Aboriginal ethnic and cultural groups in Australia, all with their own history of song and dance. Some dances celebrate the rites of passage for children to become adults, amounting to an initiation ceremony. One such

Aboriginal men provide music for the corroboree ceremony.

The corroboree is a ceremony where Aboriginals paint their bodies, play music, and dance along to demonstrate a link to the spiritual world and their ancestors.

dance that takes place among the Eora people in modern-day Sydney is called *burbung*, an initiation rite for young boys to become men of the tribe, typically by having a tooth knocked out. Women are not permitted to attend the *burbung*, although they have their own initiation rites for young girls.

Aboriginal dances serve a wide variety of cultural purposes. Most Aboriginal dances seek to tell a story, whether a creation myth or a hero's journey, that has been a crucial part of their tribal identity. Others invoke the divine to provide enough food for the community. Some dances go even further, teaching survival skills, like how to start a fire to clear brush, renewing the soil and exposing animals for hunting. Perhaps the most famous Aboriginal dance takes place during the *corroboree*, a ceremony where Aboriginals paint their bodies, play music, and dance along to demonstrate a link to the spiritual world and their ancestors. *Corroboree* dances are particularly challenging, requiring a high degree of technical precision and requiring young tribal members to learn the steps from a young age in order to succeed.

BAMBOO POLES AND TINIKLING

Many dances across the world use a variety of props and costumes, but the *tinikling* dance of the Philippines goes a step further, putting a pair of bamboo poles in the way of dancers so that they have to leap back and forth to clear the obstacle. The name is derived from a type of bird named the *tikling*, famous for being able to dodge bamboo traps set up by farmers to catch birds that eat their seeds in rice paddies. *Tinikling* is thought to have originated on the isle of Leyte at a time when the Philippines was a colony of Spain, over 100 years ago; legend holds that the dance originated when the king of Spain set a rule that Filipino workers could be punished by having their ankles whipped with bamboo poles. Rebellious workers leapt over the poles as they came in to thrash their ankles, with the movement evolving from a reaction to the challenge into a national dance.

Men and women participate in the* tinikling *dance.

While dancing the* tinikling*, dancers must be barefoot.

Today, *tinikling* is always a joy for audiences to watch, due to the amount of skill required for dancers to transverse the pair of bamboo poles without falling over them. Both men and women who dance the *tinikling* do so in full formal garments: Men wear the national outfit, an untucked collared shirt and red trousers, whereas women wear a colorful dress called a *balintawak*. Both participants are barefoot.

Dancers must listen closely to the music to synchronize their steps and avoid tripping over the bamboo poles. Both partners jump as they dance, resembling a hopscotch-like motion as they confidently move their legs and ankles upward as the bamboo handlers touch the poles together in time with the music. *Tinikling* requires a great deal of concentration: The music, the pole movement, and the partner's steps all must be taken into consideration to prevent a misstep and a trip.

Dancers perform* joget *at a festival.

JAMMING TO *JOGET* IN MALAYSIA

The most popular type of traditional dance in Malaysia, called *joget*, is thought to have originated about 400 years ago, when Portuguese colonization mixed European cultures with the indigenous Malaya culture. *Joget* is a famously lively dance with an up-tempo musical beat that keeps the dancers going at a fast pace throughout the performance. It is a partner dance that emphasizes playfulness and even humor between both participants, with physical teasing and flirtation as they go. Like other popular folk dances, *joget* most commonly comes into play during weddings, festivals, and other celebrations.

Musicians playing a violin, a gong drum, a flute, and a tambourine called a *rebana* usually accompany *joget* dancing. Musicians frequently switch from double to triple beats as they play, meaning that dancers need to be aware of alterations in tempo. What's more, participants may have to shift the weight on their feet as the tempo changes, called "ball change," as they go from having their weight on the balls of their feet to the heel.

The Malaysia Spice Trade

The introduction of European culture to Malaysia and parts of Indonesia reflects the importance of the spice trade in history. Spices grown in Oceania, like cinnamon, nutmeg, or black pepper, are difficult or even impossible to grow elsewhere, making them valuable for their rarity as well as their piquant taste. Centuries ago, trade routes connecting Malaysia to faraway European markets made traders wealthy, and European powers fought for control of these remote islands. Parts of Malaysia changed hands between the Spanish, Portuguese, Dutch, and British throughout their history; not until the aftermath of World War II did Malaysia become wholly independent from foreign influence.

GUAM'S YOUNG MAN STICK DANCE

The American-owned island of Guam in the South Pacific is a famous tourist destination, especially because American dollars are accepted and people speak English. Those who arrive will find many unique aspects of Guam culture, such as the *bailan uritao*, or "young man's dance." Accompanied by traditional Chamarro music, dancers evoke the warrior training of ancient tribes by leaping into the air, shouting, and banging together *tunas* sticks in perfect time with the music. The motion of the sticks not only evokes combat: The dance ends with all participants holding their points facing upward in a cone shape, similar to the roof of a building, demonstrating teamwork as well as martial capability.

Guam is famous for women's as well as men's dances. The *bailan lina'la'*, or "Dance of Life," is a female-only dance where the women drop in through the roof created by the men's dance, wearing coconut-leaf skirts.

Female Chamorro dancers perform the "Dance of Life."

PLAYING WITH FIRE

Few dances across the world can compare in terms of spectacle and intensity to the *baining* fire dance, native to a tribe in Papua New Guinea and most often performed after the birth of a new child in the village or for the initiation of young boys to become men and tribal leaders. Boys of the tribe light a large bonfire and then hit bamboo sticks together to create a percussion rhythm. Adult men (women are not permitted to join in the ceremony) don oversized, cartoonlike masks.

The music builds in tempo and volume until the men of the tribe are worked into a frenzy and rush through the bonfire itself. Tradition holds that the dance must go on for as long as the firewood holds out, meaning that some dances can go on throughout the night; the last things to burn are the masks themselves. The dance ends when the fire runs low enough that the men can dart in and put out the last embers with nothing more than their bare feet.

***A baining** fire dancer dons a larger cartoonlike mask while dancing around a bonfire.*

THE *HAKA* CHALLENGE

The Maori haka dance has become a notable event, especially before New Zealand sporting events.

One of the most famous dances of Oceania is the *haka*, the traditional dance performed by New Zealand's Maori natives prior to combat. Maori arrange themselves in a line and chant in a booming, aggressive manner, pounding their feet up and down to demonstrate strength. This martial dance has been adopted by New Zealand's national sports teams, most notably the All Blacks national rugby team, and is performed prior to events to intimidate the opposition. The *haka* is so popular among New Zealand sports teams that it is even done on unusual surfaces: The national hockey team has performed it on a sheet of ice!

TELLING A STORY BY *MEKE*

Meke dancers wear grass skirts and feathered armbands.

The small island of Fiji is well known as a tourist destination where the natives pride themselves on many aspects of their culture, including the *meke* dance. This dance requires nothing more than a *lali*, a Fijian drum, and a pair of hands to clap along to the beat. Dancers famously wear grass skirts and feathered armbands of multifaceted colors to draw attention to their movements. *Meke* tells a story through dance, ranging from a spear dance of warrior men to a fan dance of women, although men and women participate in both types of *meke* dances.

THE DANCING GROUNDS OF VANUATU

Vanuatu dancers.

For most cultures around the world, where you dance is much less important than how you dance. In Vanuatu, location is everything. Traditional dancing grounds, called *nasara*, provide a place for expression and ceremony among the Vanuatu tribes. They employ a drum called a *gong* (no relation to the metal gong of East Asian culture), made from a hollowed-out tree trunk, to keep the beat. It is believed to provide the voice of the spirits and the ancestors, and no other instruments are required to celebrate an occasion. The most important *nasara* is located on Tanna Island, where different tribes come together to dance and cement their friendships and alliances.

SOME MORE OF SAMOA DANCE

The Samoans are perhaps the oldest Polynesian culture that still exists today, settling on isles throughout the Pacific about 3,000 years ago. Traditional Samoan dance exists throughout various isles, most of which take the name *siva*, which simply means "dance." Samoan *siva* are famous for the bright costumes of bird feathers, boar tusks, shells, and coconut husks. The *taualaga* dance concludes a Samoan wedding, performed by the son or daughter of a village chief, and traditionally it was so important that only virgins could perform it; today, most performers are still young unmarried persons. It is a solo performance to a drumbeat.

Samoan siva.

FURTHER READING & INTERNET RESOURCES

BOOKS

Cohen, Selma Jeanne, ed. *International Encyclopedia of Dance*. Oxford, UK: Oxford University Press, 1998.
A comprehensive study of global dance, with details about a wide variety of cultures and geographical regions.

Ehrenreich, Barbara. *Dancing in the Streets: A History of Collective Joy*. New York: Metropolitan Books, 2006.
Ehrenreich's thesis is that dance reflects a movement toward happiness. Her book attempts to study how this has played out in dance history, with both progress and repression.

Jonas, Gerald. *Dancing: The Pleasure, Power, and Art of Movement*. New York: Harry N. Abrams, 1992.
A textbook on the various types of dance throughout the world. Jonas covers different places, performances, and time periods.

Novak, Cynthia. *Sharing the Dance: Contact Improvisation and American Culture*. Madison, WI: University of Wisconsin Press, 1990.
A look at the way that American dance styles have trended toward improvisation rather than orthodoxy, reflecting the changes of broader culture and politics.

Stearns, Marshall, and Jean Stearns. *Jazz Dance: The Story of American Vernacular Dance*. New York: De Capo Press, 1994.
The origins of jazz music and the dance that quickly followed; the Stearns's work looks deeper into the creation of this uniquely American art style.

Thompson, Robert Farris. *Tango: The Art History of Love*. New York: Vintage Press, 2006.
A comprehensive look at the history of tango, from its roots in Argentinian slave culture to its export throughout the wider world.

WEB SITES

allworlddance.com. All World Dance provides up-to-date news, videos, and reviews of dance in different nations and genres.

cnd.fr/en. The Web site of the French National Dance Center, this site provides resources for research, performances and exhibitions, and even practical information on how to dance particular moves.

dancecase.com. The video-hosting site Dance Case contains a large library of dances, from street funk to samba, with examples of how to perform a wide variety of different dances.

dancenotation.org. The nonprofit Dance Notation Bureau seeks to catalogue and record dance types throughout the world, providing information on footwork, rhythm, and music so that anyone can perform any dance they choose.

infinitebody.blogspot.com. This blog, run by the former professional dancer Eva Yaa Asantewaa, documents and reviews performances, trends, and artists, as well as shares news from the music and art world.

cid-portal.org/site. The International Dance Council, based out of Paris within UNESCO, is "the official umbrella organization for all forms of dance in all countries of the world." The Web site provides a directory of dances, promotes International Dance Day, and features a virtual library of resources and information.

dancemuseum.org. The Web site for the New York-based National Museum of Dance, the foremost dance museum in the United States, with news and events.

INDEX

AUTHOR'S BIOGRAPHY

David Wilson has a bachelor's degree in history from Miami University and a graduate degree in history from the University of Cincinnati. His writings on social studies have been published by educational institutes like Norwich University, Peregrine Academics, and Study.com. He lives in Denver.

CREDITS

COVER

(clockwise from top left) Navruz Festival, Los Angeles, CA, betto rodrigues/Shutterstock; Zulu tribal dance, South Africa, Irishka777/Dreamstime; flamenco dancers, Spain, Jackq/Dreamstime; dragon dance, Foshan City, China, Guangliang Huo/Dreamstime; break dancing, New York City, chaoss/Shutterstock; samba dancers, São Paulo, Brazil, Samystclair/Dreamstime

INTERIOR

1, Jackq/Dreamstime; 2–3, Dr Ajay Kumar Singh/Dreamstime; 5, Dmitry Rukhlenko/Shutterstock; 9, Polyudova Yulia/Shutterstock; 10, Debbie Aird Photography/Shutterstock; 11, Hongqi Zhang (aka Michael Zhang)/Dreamstime; 12, Obe Images/Wikimedia Commons; 13, Nicole S Glass/Shutterstock; 14, Anna Om/Dreamstime; 15, Africanway/iStock; 16, Yury Birukov/Dreamstime; 17, Fabian Plock/Dreamstime; 18, violent_strings/Shutterstock; 19, Siempreverde22/iStock; 20 (UP), Ryan M. Bolton/Shutterstock; 20 (LO), Paop/Dreamstime; 21, Ivanchina Anna/Shutterstock; 22, Readyprophotos/Dreamstime; 23, Nina Hilitukha/Dreamstime; 24, windmoon/iStock; 25, Kertu/Shutterstock; 26, Komkrit Muangchan/Dreamstime; 27, Mr. Namart Pieamsuwan/Dreamstime; 28, pattio/Wikimedia Commons; 29, Epel/Shutterstock; 30, Tatiana Chekryzhova/Shutterstock; 31 (UP), Anizza/Dreamstime; 31 (LO), jethuynh/iStock; 32 (UP), Ritesh Chaudhary/Shutterstock; 32 (LO), Saiko3p/Dreamstime; 33, CSA Images/iStock; 34, kamienczanka/Shutterstock; 35, Tokomag/Dreamstime; 36, Henri de Gissey/Wikimedia Commons; 37, Igor Bulgarin/Shutterstock; 38, PobladuraFCG/iStock; 39, Mengtianhan/Dreamstime; 40, Jackq/Dreamstime; 41, Roberto Galan/Shutterstock; 42, Vladvitek/Dreamstime; 43 (UP), Inacio Pires/Dreamstime; 43 (LO), Pderrett/iStock; 44 (UP), Outesticide/Wikiemedia Commons; 44 (LO), Marcus Ramberg/Wikimedia Commons; 45, draco77vector/Shutterstock; 46, Celso Pupo Rodrigues/Dreamstime; 47, Samystclair/Dreamstime; 48, Kobby Dagan/Shutterstock; 49, Alexandre Fagundes De Fagundes/Dreamstime; 50, Golden_Brown/iStock; 51, Mauro_Repossini/iStock; 52, Daniel Romero/Newscom; 53, Marcelodlt/Shutterstock; 54, Germán Falcón/Newscom; 55 (UP), peeterv/iStock; 55 (LO), Ozphotoguy/Shutterstock; 56 (UP), Garry Knight/Wikimedia Commons; 56 (LO), Solarisys13/Dreamstime; 57, Sahas2015/Shutterstock; 58, HansMusa/Shutterstock; 59, HansMusa/Shutterstock; 60, Altosvic/Shutterstock; 61, Kobby Dagan/Dreamstime; 62, Sujay_Govindaraj/iStock; 63, Sergey Lyashenko/Shutterstock; 64, Bilai Jawich/Newscom; 65, betto rodrigues/Shutterstock; 66, U Creative Photography/Shutterstock; 67 (UP), Jeremy Brown/Dreamstime; 67 (LO), Meganesia/Wikimedia Commons; 68 (UP), Sarah Canbel/Wikimedia Commons; 68 (LO), Fatih Polat/Dreamstime; 69, Aleutie/Shutterstock; 70, Goran Bogicevic/Shutterstock; 71, plus99/iStock; 72, Thomas Carter/Dreamstime; 73, Thomas Carter/Dreamstime; 74, lev radin/Shutterstock; 75, lev radin/Shutterstock; 76, Pius Lee/Dreamstime; 77, Frame 18 Productions/Shutterstock; 78, MPH Photos/Shutterstock; 79 (UP), Wikimedia Commons; 79 (LO), Roberto Galan/Shutterstock; 80 (UP), Glasshouse Images/Newscom; 80 (LO), Che/Wikimedia Commons; 81, Incomible/Dreamstime; 82, Garudeya/Dreamstime; 83, Garudeya/Dreamstime; 84, Philip Schubert/Shutterstock; 85, Philip Schubert/Shutterstock; 86, Tony Magdaraog/Shutterstock; 87, U.S. Airforce, Senior Airman Nestor Cruz/Wikimedia Commons; 88, Ravindran John Smith/Dreamstime; 89, Marilyn Sourgose/Wikimedia Commons; 90, Taro Taylor/Wikimedia Commons; 91 (UP), ChameleonsEye/Shutterstock; 91 (LO), Nadezda Zavitaeva/Shutterstock; 92 (UP), Lizgiv/Dreamstime; 92 (LO), Rico Leffanta/Dreamstime